VESTIGES

VESTIGES

Poems by

Mercedes Lawry

Cover design by Shay Culligan
Cover art by CJ Young

ISBN: 978-1-63980-239-5

Kelsay Books
502 South 1040 East, A-119
American Fork, Utah 84003
Kelsaybooks.com

For Dan, now fishing in the sky

Acknowledgments

2River: "Low Maintenance," "Muscle Memory"

AJI Magazine: "Surface"

Alaska Quarterly Review: "Sky Rabble"

Barrow Street: "I Meet a Man"

Bellingham Review: "Immobile Movement," "This one thing became another and another"

Blue Earth Review: "Between the tree and the sky"

Caliban: "After Zero, One," "In the Journey, the Relinquishing"

Catamaran Literary Reader: "Spring Indeterminate"

Cider Press Review: "The Wry Scientist"

Cirque: "Lighting Out from the Failed Homestead," "Dusk"

Cobalt: "A Fine Line to Lunacy"

Constellations: "Winter Coping Skills"

Gold Man Review: "Wall," "We Broke Apart"

Harpur Palate: "I implore the bat"

Hawaii Pacific Review: "Flu Shot"

HEArt: "Little Appetites"

Helen: "How to Live: An Option"

Ilanot Review: "Mouth"

Innisfree Poetry Journal: "You must put it into words"

Isthmus: "December"

Janus Head: "As Night Falls to Morning: An Interior Monologue"

Kestrel: "I fancy myself in a blues moment"

Kettle Blue Review: "Relative to Everything," "Such Reasons Made Manifest"

Kudzu House Quarterly: "Not Thought Strange"

The Lake: "Haydn's Floating Heads"

Moss: A Journal of the Pacific Northwest: "Lily, Dimmed"

Natural Bridge: "Passage"

Nimrod: "Allow"

ONE: "Bad Companion"

Pittsburgh Poetry Review: "Me & Big Pharma"

Poetry Northwest: "Ferlinghetti at the Rotary Club"

Posit: "Extinction"

Quiddity: "Clearing"
Salamander: "Put forth for consideration"
SAND: "Exit Strategy"
Southword Journal: "I Tell You This, My Termagant"
St. Ann's Review: "Mad March as Such"
Superstition Review: "From the Corner of an Eye"
Switched-on Gutenberg: "The Hill," "When is it luck? When is it accident," "In Concert with Yearning"
Tampa Review: "I am satisfied with weeds"
The Fourth River: "A Civil War Tale"
Theodate: "In the Early Garden with Reason"
Tulane Review: "Shallow End"
Two Hawks Quarterly: "False Flight"
Valparaiso Review: "Eye Exam"
Verdad Magazine: "What is said and what is not said and where that leaves us"
Weber—The Contemporary West: "Echo," "Options in Diverse Territory," "Ascending Blue"

SPECIAL THANKS to two women who are gone now but greatly influenced and supported my work—Beth Bentley and Marilyn Zuckerman. Thanks also to Carol V. Davis, Eileen Duncan, Sherry Rind, Alicia Hokanson, Anne Pitkin, Mim Harrison, and Patty Cannon whose love of language and moral support have been so important, especially during these last several surreal years.

Contents

III

I

A Fine Line to Lunacy

Greedy September edges me
toward precipice, toward winter-dim hunger.

A spent blue sky tenders solace,
and later, the blood moon floods

the black plate of night, teasing,
as if this were a miracle instead of

science. I climb into bed, troubled,
anxious for the blankness to descend

while the red echo, like a rescue light,
winks out of the fog of stalled memory.

I curl as tightly as I can,
thinking I, too, might make a moon,

only waning, sliver by gilded sliver,
until I am finally new.

Immobile Movement

Swimming in a Miro sky,
my fingers trace waves, spirals,
curled creatures and *colors like words.*
I beg you,
do not pull me down or utter prayers.
Let me navigate,
wind loosening my bones
as I become every blue,
deep dark to pallid ink.
And you can remember me
in the sea or the Lenten rose,
in the bruised shadows of mountains,
in the eyes of ghost children,
in the blood routes humming beneath skin,
in the ice-choked river plain,
in the fleet wings of migrating birds,
in the shards of stars truckling down
to rest on the shoulder of dune grass,
in *the greater bareness.*

Note: Italicized phrases are taken from quotes by Joan Miro

Exit Strategy

Inside the blue ruin,
a degree of calm as open hand
strums frayed connection.

The ragged iris lean, less in defiance,
more as battered survivors.

The stubborn wind offers no clues, no
respite, no summary. April moves
in fits and starts, at times with a brazen sting.

The stray dog is once again snarling in the road.
There is no belonging, only hours collapsed.
Go to the back wall, I think, and climb.
Take care for the violets.

Winter Coping Skills

Hypnotizing sky, warrens
of November gray, I'm dazed
in a dark sense, cold
and damp fed up with the gloom.
It runs like lead in my veins.
It saps my already minimal spirit.
It affirms my decisions of despair.

I'll watch *Borgen* and escape
into Danish cheekbones and the puzzle
of their politics. I'll read
and feed my Anglophilia,
behind-the-scenes of Masterpiece Theatre.

Minutia that topples sanity
but makes ourselves ourselves.
A friend's mother, slowly losing memory,
hated lettuce salads for years until
that click or tick of synapse.
How much do I love my sadness
and what does it look like in bright light?
Is it mine, all mine?

In the Journey, the Relinquishing

A sun blaze made it difficult to see.
I was heading west where forgetting
might take shape, where the small darts
of pain might be abolished by a new sky.

There were no roots trailing in my wake.
Occasionally I paused in shadow while my breathing
settled. I chose to believe flight was courage.
The crusts of my hands clenched and released
as if rosary beads were slipping through. As if
I hadn't tossed prayer in the rubbish
in a year I can't now remember.

Movement of one sort can focus the mind.
It was too late to be sorry, and I'd grown sick
of stale stories, unfinished, of myths
and miracles and last-ditch rescues.

I could almost smell the salty ocean air.
It appeared my legs would hold out.
I looked forward to lying down in the whiskery
dune grass, to the swoop of pelicans
with their croaky cries and a felted night sky
punctured by stars.

Flu Shot

I talk about Ian Fleming
and James Bond.
He talks about *Lord of the Rings,*
the movie, gently pinches
my arm and stabs.
Fleming had a talent for intelligence and sex
and I read his books
on the sly, as did my brother
who procured them until
my mother confiscated *The Spy Who Loved Me*
before he'd read it and now
he's dead and I have no idea
if he ever did read it.
My arm goes sore. The vaccine
moves inside me like a dozen rivers.
The pharmacist loves his movies.
When we were children, my brother and I
were friendly. Then, we weren't.

Me and Big Pharma

I've added a pill.
My heart beats ever harder,
short term, the doctor says.
Will the dark swallow me
less frequently? Smother
with a gentler hand?
I'm all for the placebo effect.
Whatever might usher me away
from the edge. Apparently,
I'm not yet ready to jump.
I picture the circuits in my brain
changing course with these new
signals, shadowed routes retreating,
furrows growing deeper.
It's not that I think there is a fix
for sadness. I just want a tougher skin,
closer to pineapple, less like plum.

I Tell You This, My Termagant

Toodle on, termagant,
my sister-soul, the mossy bottom layer
of myself. Play out enigmas
and discord; wink, wink,
your wry and cheeky sense wriggling
laughs out of the very ones who cluck
at your dark palisades. Part snake
with a zippity tongue, sharp words spit
in a hiss-threat when you're only aiming
at unadorned truth. Few like that.

Now, the body resembles spirit, furrowed,
saggy, plum bruised and a general sinking.
We are heading down, little termagant,
back to the parched earth so confused by misrule
it may not want us any longer.
We'll freshen our scowls and survey
the remains, for we're nothing if not on target,
rings around the moon notwithstanding.

Lighting Out from the Failed Homestead

He started down the wagon road. The early dew
was still excitable, a stir in the air
borrowed from dawn. He passed
a foul sink of rainwater at the bottom of the hill
and fields where ravens pestered sky.
He'd left his brothers in the graves,
the empty house and stubborn echoes.
Adrift in the world now. Untethered.
He knew to say little and show gratitude.
This was a new country with old secrets.
If there was luck beyond the ridge, so be it.
He might be dead in a week or so.
He might be whistling and welcoming stars
and a fat river that revealed plenty of stones
so the crossing would be easy and he could sip
the cold water and let it run over his face
and feel the worth of moving on.

How to Live: An Option

He was a renegade
and she was a renegade's lover
and soon, there were little renegades,
cute as the dickens.
He had flair and nerve
and a fine set of muscles.
She was lanky and leaned on him
for all things practical and more.
They were often on the run.
They were good runners,
even the little ones with their short legs.
He did not fit in and now, neither
did she and certainly not the little ones,
though they'd have a chance, later,
to reform. He had a plan
and she trusted his plan
and the little ones had no idea about plans,
nor should they, at their ages.
They moved through the world
and right there, over their shoulders,
the world was showing its fangs.

I Meet a Man

He came from a place he called an estuary town.
He had a fine voice. It was the first thing I noticed.
He asked me questions about myself. Thoughtful.

I began to tell him things and soon, it was as if
I had given myself to him, without touching.
He caused me to laugh. He allowed for that space.

I was unsettled at this time. I could have gone
or stayed, it mattered little. I had no reasons
in my pockets or in my heart. I could not dissemble.

He appeared to be free of such tussles.
I asked him about his town, was it a place
to return to? Might I be happy there?

He couldn't say, of course he couldn't say.
We'd only met and here I was, probing for rescue.
I could travel there, to the estuary town, and see for myself.

He'd draw me a map. He'd point out a few sights.
I might go, I told him, and I might not.
I said this as if I was a devil-may-care girl.

I fancy myself in a blues moment

The light was bad
for a broken heart.
I was ripped apart
and useless, half full
of cheap beer
and bruised oranges.
God, I wish I smoked
and the stars would stay
behind clouds. I just
want a porch with shadows
and a Mississippi dream.
I just want the same thing
I had a week ago
and a bucket of forgiveness.

Low Maintenance

The loose step at the bottom
has rotted through, saturated
with winter rains. Now propped
on bricks, wedged into dirt,
not worth repair because
the whole damn porch has gone
to hell and I'm taking the long view
on total collapse. The house
is a bucket of wounds and ruin.
I'm gambling on which of us goes first.
But the tulips are bold this year,
all scarlet stripes and blood reds.
And the pear tree still fills
with milky blooms even though
I hacked the branches that were reaching
like tentacles toward the wires,
averting one more domestic disaster,
that could have given the high sign
to the wrecking ball.

Wall

I tried scrambling over the wall
but it's too slick, too fraught
with alibis and clever narratives
that spill their guts so you find yourself
weeping and unable to get a toehold.

Damn, I said, damn this wall
that makes us all nervous and willing
to placate their holier-than-thou majesties
just so we can get a cold potato
and keep the photo of our dead dog
under our worn-down pillows
as if that was a high sign for compassion.

I tried more than once to climb over
that wall, in the early morning fog,
when the babies are starting to murmur,
in the hollow night when every dream
has packed up and jumped ship,
in a blinding rain, thinking I might swim over
on a miracle flood, in an early June wind
that could preoccupy anyone with its sweet pretense.

We have forgotten what's on the other side of the wall,
but we haven't forgotten what the sun looks like
when it falls into the black sea or what happens to seeds
when you plant them in the earth
and give them light and water.

Bruises bloom on my fingers, over
my wrists. Some days I lean against the wall
with empty thoughts. Most days I try again,
time whittled needle-thin
beneath fresh wounds.

You Must Put It into Words

Blah blah blah, said the dog.
The crow was not happy about it.
The cat napped.
The raccoon longed for a cigarette.
The duck refused to acknowledge anyone.
The chicken would not shut up.
Blah blah blah, the dog repeated.
Thus, the weeks rolled on without refreshment.
On certain days the wind was fierce,
creating a heightened nervousness.
For some, this was a welcome change.
It was only when the dog failed to speak
that the rest became concerned about syllables,
articulation, diction, proper nouns
and the loss of control resulting from the babel.
Finally, another stepped forward and said
blah blah blah with almost the same gusto,
though he wore a mask and could not be identified.
The sense of relief was palpable
and life went on, fervent and ironic.

As Night Falls to Morning: An Interior Monologue

I was told the bail bondsman was not coming back.
A blue slice of midnight sat on my plate,
uneaten. The little ones were quiet now.
I tore up the family history in as many small pieces
as I could, before my fingers gave up.
The reckless twin shows an affinity for music.
I can hope, loving the piano as I do.
The doors are locked, front and back
and there is no wind to rattle the shutters.
This is my best thinking time. I assess
my situation which continues, in some ways,
the same, lonely as that may be. But winter
is next and I just don't know how much
teeth chattering I can take. We need
another quilt. He told me himself at the moment
of departure. Others had told me earlier.
Warnings, they called it, as if I was stupid.
When I am stupid, it's because I choose to be.
I think I'll make a pie, a pie under the stars,
what a pretty thing. A pie filled with the breath
of babies and whatever I can conjure.
What a fine idea. I set to it.

From the Corner of an Eye

The Duke of Urbino suffered the loss of an eye
in a tournament. This mishap had several
consequences, but perhaps most crucial to his good health
was the lessening of peripheral vision.

Try it. Close one eye and look to the opposite side
and what do you see? Your nose.
With both eyes open, the nose disappears.
I learn this in an essay by Lawrence Wechsler.

Back to the Duke, a condottieri who was living
in a time of nasty intrigue, conspirators lurking
in hallways and spies spilling out of secret doors.
This Duke is said to have inspired Machiavelli,
so we understand he was no slouch at ruse and deception.
He feared, however, with his impaired sight,
he might miss the flash of sword, a shadow
easing out from the tapestry and to address this danger,
had the bridge of his nose shaved off.

Wechsler was concerned with perspective in art
but I am taken with this mercenary who detected how
a diminished snout would enhance his chances.
With an angular profile, he lived a long, if bloody, life.

Haydn's Floating Heads

Buried first with a "substitute" skull,
Joseph Haydn lost his head to fanatics
of phrenology who hoped to link his musical genius
to an appropriate bump. Though located later,
it was not until 1954 that head was reconciled to body,
re-buried with the stand-in head perhaps as reward
or nod to its consecration and reluctance to chuck it into a bin.

As bits and pieces of saints are scattered
in dim chapels and damp naves, the body parts of the renowned
sometimes achieve a life of their own. The holiness
of a Haydn head spans years like a rosary of rogue notes.
Where does music live and how does it escape idea?
Curling out from the splendid folds and fissures
inside a pocket of bone.

The Hill

Quick-winged in a chrysalis of shadow,
she and he went up the hill
with vague agendas aside from vista,
the heady lift that came with ascension,
removal from slog and bog and bitter roots.

She and he went up the hill
with sketchy motives aside from frisson
of elevation, escape from chatter and natter
and wounded glances, into a tender silhouette,
a refuge, a pristine cocoon.

With something resembling love, though not fully,
at times false, at times, diminished,
she and he went up the hill,
and thick with the unsettled and suspicious,
were depleted by a constant shift in trust.

Lust flared at odd moments and might again
on a peak with a rumpus of wind.
The tremble of flesh might again ring from touch.
Breath might again catch and shiver, when
she and he went up the hill.

Or they might each be consumed entire
by exhaustion, this romantic scrabble
taking a toll that left them with little choice so that
she and he went up the hill
and neither, neither came down.

A Civil War Tale

"Bring me the anatomy book."
is not a sentence you want to hear
if you're lying on a cold, kitchen table
with no morphine for a hundred miles,
blood oozing from your ripped skin
where bone slivers out, askew and taunting,
and a glinting saw rests in the hands
of a tall, grim woman who is not queasy
or put off by a difficult task, who
likely does not regard you with any
compassion beyond the minimal
that might or might not keep you alive,
you being the enemy after all,
a woman who has tended muscles
and flesh, limbs and sinews,
attached, re-attached, who shot
a lame horse without pause,
who may or may not share the diminishing
whiskey for which you'd gladly
sell your tarnished soul and any
first born child that waits in the clouds,
a woman of spare beauty with all the power.

Note: "Bring me the anatomy book." is a line from the film "Beguiled"

Ferlinghetti at the Rotary Club

Gary and I read Ferlinghetti
at the Rotary Club in 1969. *Christ
climbed down* and so on.
This was arranged by Mr. Metz,
A.P. teacher in the fledgling days.
Short, fussy man with a spitfire brain and snarky tongue
who lived with his mother as the times dictated.
We were embarrassed by the men in sad suits
oozing bonhomie and aftershave,
so "establishment", when we were trying hard
to become hippies. They wouldn't have a clue
 how to find *A Coney Island of the Mind.*
At least it was Ferlinghetti, pocked
with West Coast anarchy, free love and patchouli,
which suggests there was a wild river and *a rebirth of wonder*
running beneath the Pittsburgh suburbs.

II

The Wry Scientist

The wry scientist feels heroics are unnecessary.
She shirks the convoluted equations and heads
for the atomic heart. The orbit of thought sliced
by need, dissected by a frivolous narrative
and neatly stacked by the bed. Hence, dreams
without effort. Little bird feet tick tacking
on a page, the world is a cage, is a series of
clashing explanations like greens, winter,
spring, what grows and dies to a sad, skint twig.
She is no mother of mercy. She is no shrill Cassandra.
Let's all spin, she thinks, till we fall down,
proving a point in the garbled scheme of the world.

Surface

High and sweet, the sparrow trills,
glissando on wind before soft rain.
The pallor of a boy in a damp country,
the glisten, as if stories brimmed
beneath skin, the insides threshing
at muted sky. Nothing of sorrow
sticks in the branches of the hawthorn.
Nothing of regret. The boy is a muddle,
chancing little with his musings.
His long fingers needle the leaves
as he keeps watch. Perhaps his truth
will emerge from the gray layers,
sporting its own wings and clever eyes.
Such hopes whistle at the edge of an hour
He strings them together like shiny beads.

Shallow End

Fear is a rook and a tendril,
a vacant cup, a cinnamon thief,
a frayed hysteric.

Polluted waters fester and froth
and anyone voyaging forth will begin
to lose heart.

No river or lake or wide ghost-sea
where little pieces of the damned
can be swallowed.

Just this: wary, wounded,
hands reaching for the surface
in the wavy blue cathedral.

Between the tree and the sky

Black wing flat against blue, sudden.
The man with an illness, gaunt
as a twig, lifts toward the sky.
The bird hurries at the wind, a silhouette,
a dagger of death here and away.
The man cradles his sickness, body
with no boundary. His arms encircle the tree.
He asks the empty blue and then, the bird,
passing, unaware. Between this life
as the man knows it and the end of it.
As if birds might determine,
or one dark bird, fracturing the sky.
The ruin of the man is soon forgotten
as failure wipes clean the bones,
the feathers, the blood, the mossy bark.

Little Appetites

Pretty and forgiving,
little girl down the road
needing shoes and bread.
Wind scooping at the roof,
holes here and there
like bird mouths open
to worms. Daddy
licking at the bottle,
gone inside his dead heart.
Old bluetick under
the porch, given up
and swollen. Picture
this and plenty more
all over the hills,
in the towns and thick
in city stink and everywhere
hunger knows its way
into soft child bellies.

After Zero, One

Shown to be a slice of particular measure
framed as construct, named
as hour or minute. In the hands of the man
at roof's edge, maybe paper
with mundane word, or gospel
or small white field.
Do birds take notice or mimic
curiosity? The man might have forgotten
the weight of bread crusts. Never
fed the birds, studied wings, or cared to.
Ribbed clouds skim to the east.
He is counting now, silently.
Numbers will fall, too, and become nothing.
The time spent contemplating.
The decision. The time spent going down.

Relative to Everything

What's a dark morning
in your scheme of things,
a bowl of sour plums,
a faint psalm-memory, a forgotten
pair of shoes shoved under the bed?
What's the swipe of silk around your neck,
a salt grain, a five-course meal,
or the waddle of pimped art?

The hungry are still outside, calling.
The heroes are scratching names on rock,
burying fast and fevered.
The dogs are wherever they want,
coddled or cursed.
The winners need not worry.
The losers need not hope.
You think you can negotiate
with goodness, pockets overflowing.
But soft nights harbor thin blades
disguised as stars.
Sleep well, my deary dear,
until you won't.

Passage

She passed through the interrupted light,
the strange yellow light.
She knew nothing in the morning
but by night, everything. The roots
of trees buckled the sidewalks
causing dangerous mosaics. She believed fools
often had the last word, which made her
nervous. The books she'd finished stacked
by the door. Her keys in the copper bowl.
Her bruised arms, both blue and yellow,
each bruise tender and evolving.

Such Reasons Made Manifest

Because I have a skeleton, I am greedy for bread.
Because the wind enters my ears and wreaks havoc
on my equilibrium, I cannot sing in tune.
Because there are so many greens to choose from,
I choose blue.

First, the racket of hail, a minor assault on the house,
a vestigial thrill in the gray collapse.
Next, streaks of orange and pocked clouds.
Then, stillness, all but a testy crow.

Because I swallow an emphasis on pause.
Because the apple tree has branches to spare
and the roots, too, are generous.
Because lies have left scars and I have a tendency
to worry them.

The frescoes emerge inside my eyelids.
Remnants of wings attach at my heels.
I carry the blather like a bowl of soup
and its steam burns my fingers,
clouds my vision.

Sky Rabble

Outside, an ascension of raspy crows.
On the windowsill, two blue bottles arc
light over a scatter of stiff insects.
In the spare pause of an October afternoon,

I am counting up the dead, the years a fog
and too exhausting to decipher. Gone
is gone. The house is empty, and I like it now,
my thoughts in chaos and unfettered.

The spindly apple tree shivers and bows,
red orbs hanging by a thread, shriveling.
Behind, the great gold leaves of the maple
come down in noisy cascades
when a brisk wind slices through.

I am diminishing at a steady pace.
Winter is harder to endure.
The gates are closing. I pay attention
to the birds now, their scoot and flit
across the woolen sky.

Extinction

Less the skim of moon than a whimper
as the swallows of early evening leave us
naked with our stale despair.
A haunted blue settles into black,
the edge of trees, a jagged saw, a risky
silhouette, the ways the human
can evaporate. *Tsk tsk*
of nightbirds like a slow crawl
into our thoughts which shift with the dissipation
of light, so that shape becomes elusive,
unbordered and we can see how
easy it is to disappear, how little
that means to the pines and the firs and the heron
carving its way east.

We Broke Apart

A ruin of clouds gave us
pause, as if we'd forgotten
about chapters, coyly titled as clues.
Nothing is as abrupt as disappointment.
We observed the fields of switchgrass and chickory,
longing for a further reach, the sky roiling
in blue-black hurt. I gave you
the last chance, with tenderness.
We wore the coming rain as departure
though I still imagined another year
cluttered with sorrow, yet familiar.

Here in the depths of September,
we break apart with no loud crack,
although it seems my bones are separating
as though an alphabet was fractured
into unattached letters, spelling only Babel.

In Concert with Yearning

The Jacques Prévert poster skims above the mantel,
flanked by my altar to the dead: bears and frogs,
ashes and candles, the Balinese puppet.
Dust is thick but somehow holy,
if it's not just my laziness, which is unequivocal.
The heat of the day slowly builds and layers
the house, pinning me like a specimen moth.
As the central figure in the Prévert,
a girl, paused gingerly on a tightrope
tilted down, holds a long balance pole with arrowed tip.
Surrounded by the busyness of the world, she's focused
on the wire, the pinhole at the end, else she might find herself
a commemoration, a shiny silver figure
keeping company with my husband (pictured), on the rugged
Northwest coast, and my mother (pictured), both
with walking sticks in hand. They no longer need to watch their
    step.
They've fallen, in the same stunned year.
They fell like wings released.

Echo

Small birds as echo.
Ruin now familiar.

Ache as definition,
       transitive

I spar with death as other
craving balance. Don't forget

the gracious blue sky.
       Oh, moment of breath.

You have no grave.
Should I apologize?

       Confused by the hours,
       how they move.

How I cannot, at times,
move or wish to.

Muscle Memory

Wasn't the cool shell of my belly
a place of sweet repose? Did I dream that?
Wasn't there tenderness in the way our feet
barely touched in sleep?
Time turns odd, stretching like elastic
only to snap back, quick, with a sting.
I don't know if I'm waiting for dusk
or slipping into the seams of the hours.
I hold fast to the harbor we once made,
muscle and bone entwined, breath
rivering our skin. This remains,
in the strange ways grief grows old:
I felt safe and tethered to the world.

Clearing

At the mouth of the river, light sieves
through clouds while pelicans stutter onto small waves.
Grief is shapeless, uncontained by sky
or fevered efforts, by elements or consolation.

Along the trail, false Solomon's seal, salal, humps
of sword ferns, all thorns of memory
that do not evaporate or scurry
under rocks coated in dark sand.

Across the water is tribal land.
Another loss rustles through those trees.
Men move toward skiffs winking in a stripe of sun,
trailing nets. They make ready to fish.

What I have now is the idea of you
and a lingering doubt of the eternal.
As if these past dozen years were a slant
measure of time, strange and vaporous.

Darkness subverts boundaries,
the salve of early morning's lull,
leaves me a pilgrim
without faith or destination.

I am no closer to recognizing the fit of myself
in the world, stuck in the ecotone, life and death
easing into each other like the river and the sea,
rush and pause.

Grief is invasive, with deep, woody roots
that web into every corner of the forest.
Armed with only a trowel and secateurs,
I dig and cut, dig and cut.

Put forth for consideration

The darkness in the room
has no tongue. Each
of the half-dreams that came
with the drowse contained
an element of fear. The day
was ending. The question remained:
how to be alone? It was not only
a question, but a sentence,
a declaration, the pause
between two equal truths.

Insects nestle in the cracks,
ticking off hours.
The fire gently subtracts.
It is tame and not apocalyptic.
A November rose sucks water
from the vase while the wind
speaks in yellow particles.
Equations bring no comfort.
The little birds do their best.
She would marry the bear
if only he would come home.

III

I implore the bat

My dear bat, creature of sweet ferocity,
unfolded threat in wing-stirred air, dark
cloak, sip of night, how one dips and then another,
you and I, as if fearful, senses taut.
Oh little black thing, little horrid face,
little shim of stealth, take my disappointments
out beyond the trees, beyond hunger and grief
and the stiff lies of the duplicitous moon.

Not Thought Strange

There was a time when the classification of plant or animal
was unclear. Common belief held that a number of things
straddled both, not just in folk myth or superstition
but in such learned texts as *Histoire Admirable des Plantes*
by Claude Duet. It is the borametz that charms me,
a plant from which grew tiny, perfect lambs at the end of stems.
Allegedly found on the steppes of central Asia, with fleece
renowned for softness, the lambs were attached at the navel
and could bend down to graze around the plant until food was no
    more
and they died. A primary danger was the wolf,
who found these gentle lambs so tasty. Here was a carousel of
    young flesh
unable to flee. The brutal and the tender,
how we like our science, spiked with story.

In the Early Garden with Reason

How did that one huge fist
of a cloud form, alone
in the empty sky? What is weather
but a moment in time
surrounded by atmospheric jazz,
a roil of ions, collision and hiss?

I am sometimes in awe
and sometimes puzzled.
There is no telling what will shake you up.
March wrestled itself in
trailing webs of frost.
I take cold comfort in the crocus,
plum and yellow, moon-white,
in the emerging green furls.

How does this stack up against
the scofflaws flapping their greedy hands?
You pay attention or you don't.
You plant the early peas and the onions,
knowing the slugs are making their way.
You swallow the cold wind and are glad of it.

Lily, Dimmed

If the lily is wounded by rain,
petals collapsed to blurred alabaster,
splendor now sagging,
though more tender in its diminishment,
you might reflect on the notion of time
in the botanical world, which will fuse
with time known to a bee, or a crane fly,
a hummingbird, even the stray cat
roaming for prey. And if you
are the gardener toiling in the dirt
with a sore back and an abundance of hope,
you may see the dimmed lily
as unfortunate or ephemeral,
though probably cyclic, even beautiful
like wet paper made with cotton
or papyrus or mulberry leaves.

Options in Diverse Territory

The respectable insects remain outdoors
cherishing the plethora of flora.

The imbecilic insects steal inside
risking death by poison or resounding smack.

Neither population takes note of sirens
or incessant alarms. Only birdsong and pipe gurgle.

Creatures claim space on the porch and windowsill.
Tenuous dreaming.

The characters of earth move about
ungainly or sleek, lumbering or clipped.

Purpose in mandible or wing, hunger or song.
The fictions we swear by.
The science we imagine.

December

With a shudder of wind, the storm stops,
soothes into the wick of blue.
Birds relax, as do the maples, the shiny pine.
Brown leaves beckon past crooked bark.
Dark drumming at an early hour
folds us in and away.
Spells of softened grief linger still,
despite the years, time swimming
with no regard and steadier than anything
we might conjure as comfort.
Sky washed deeper than absence
on this Saturday, just soup
on the stove in lulling simmer
and piano tinkling from the old radio,
the sound a bit tinny but true.

I am satisfied with weeds

green frenzy, blasts of red, yellow,
however they bloom, seeking
dominion or just lush expansion.
Runners and roots, creeping, seeding,
unafraid, weeds roam the backyard
like invaders and I acquiesce.
Oh yes, I envy the gorgeousness
of minor taming, the English garden,
say, mixing, melding, just a nod
to wilderness met with the domestic.
But here I am surrounded by plants
that take what they need, classify them
as you will. They prompt frowns,
tetchy judgment from the geranium-tidy neighbors,
but I delight in such affront,
luxuriate in their grip and fierce persistence,
roving vines, deceptive tendrils,
holding onto the earth with such ferocity,
as if they knew the diggers and the pruners,
the clippers and the mowers were waiting
anxiously, just beyond the hedge.

Spring Indeterminate

The green odes of late May deceive us,
summoning hope which is sometimes
but a thief in the night.
We are safest with rain abundant
and no need to peer past trees
close to the house, hearing
roof patter, window plinks.
Out back, a blue cacophony
wild with echoes and nerve:
columbine, campanula, foxglove,
bells and rampant stars
above the old leaves from fall, now
blackened, crumbling, housing
fat worms in the sweet rot.

Dusk

Crows cross
the linen of evening,
bruising the air
with bossy squawks.

Pink threads
the blotted clouds.
The day's fretting
begins to blur.

Soon sleep will dull
the barbs
as the moon glints
like a pearly bone.

Ascending Blue

Rain's brief bruise. You know and don't know
without summary or gift. Tree-green
and a clutch as the fields recede to forest.
Dot . . . dot . . . dot . . . the sentence caught by a phrase,
a guttural gasp. Words held back. How the trail meanders,
boulders blued by disappearing light. You go up . . . step, step,
grazing rock and slurry as if the ancients had not died in their
    tracks
and you were free of their false wisdom,
your own specious regrets.

Mad March as Such

I've lost my graven image.
The tic tac of cold rain on the window
spells out insanity,
a particular kind, the 'early March
little green shoots pretending it will be all right' kind,
the 'birds with overactive imaginations in a party mode
on my roof' kind, the 'Lenten drudge of the house's
peeling paint and where is the money coming from' kind.

Upstairs, on a shelf with other religious memorabilia,
sits my missal. Paper as thin as new skin,
all those holy words, that Latin.
I might have been a mystic, flailing my arms,
if anyone had listened or propped me up.
Oh, what is spring for if not false hope?

Allow

Do not give me paraphrase.
Do not settle and sift,
leave me without recourse,
my brick tears stacking a wall.

Allow chinks where light
might ooze in. Allow syllables
to muster and cling, find
sense and delicious nonsense, both.

Do not feign or tell me tales
so tall they tickle the clouds.
Do not pretend there is love in the room.
The spin has sucked out all the air.

Let time be threaded with more
than lies, perhaps a measure of music,
or seeds for columbine and rue.
Allow me scissors for the fossil moon.
Allow me vestiges and folly.

What is said and what is not said and where that
leaves us

If the happiness factor were dressed
in something old-fashioned, something
suggesting the pioneer spirit, say,
a sunbonnet, could we find each other
more easily in a crowd or in the dark
of a broody Saturday night where nobody
was taking bets on you or me
and the dried grasses of mid-September
might light up a firestorm
with very little effort? What do you want
from a winter of extraordinary rains
and what do I want from thin arms
that cannot lift the dead dog?
Here we are at the brim, where the canny crows
sit and wait, revealing nothing aside
from their black, brainy selves. Here we are,
and wouldn't you know, one of us needs to find
a word before the ghosts forget who we are.

This one thing became another and another

In the laboratory of art,
a secret language took form.
The animals stepped
from their cages as a shim of moon
prowled the high windows.
The paintings on the wall
were echoes and rain
and errant explorers.
The wings that had been folded on shelves
opened in a slow stir of dust.
Voices unfroze and a beautiful chaos of sound
filled every space while the unlikely imaginings
faded to stories, familiar and heroic.
This was the end of hypotheses.
Every manner of blue became a sky,
a lyric rescue
a sly verb.

Mouth

Little man, little vinegar man travels
down the wrinkled river. In sight,
the osprey in a glint between trees.
The fortunate line the banks
and the less fortunate cling to boulders.
Little sour man has nothing left
in his canvas bag. No benedictions, no wise
or pithy sentences. Morning haze mocks
escape but as the day lengthens,
brittle blue fingers ease the hours
and a slow confusion shows its bones,
for how would he know when the river
finally bleeds into sea, with no one to remark it.

Bad Companion

Liar says grass yellow.
So it be before it's dead,
roots curled and brittle.
Says no rot in the back porch.
We see down to the old tin buckets
full of rain's echoes.
Liar goes high over the bent tree,
tells us this is flying. We scratch
our heads, confused. Where are wings?
We walk among false
Solomon seal, delicate as little
birds seeking insects tunneled
in moss. Liar gives us a reason
to escape the ruined Saturday
we knew would separate into jagged
pieces by nightfall when we might
rue these hours spent with Liar.
Now we hope for forgiveness
from those who cautioned.
Liar is pretty, his words pretty.
We want to swallow them with no
choking, spit them out our own selves.

False Flight

The calm lunatics don their winding sheets
and take to the streets to proclaim
the inevitable, to sing requiems
with tender fervor, to sweep their brooms
at life's debris, tick, tick, the dried leaves
of loss and the wayward, crippled love
and fear, both faint and staggering.

The calm lunatics with stanzas in their eyes,
apologies on tongues, fictions spooled
in their ears. They come singly and in crowds,
with circling hawks and honeybees.
Take their chances with the scarred moon.
Little wings rest on their shoulders, fallen
from god-knows-where. Those wings
lift slightly with each soft pause of wind.

Note: I came across the phrase "calm lunatics" in an essay in Mary Ruefle's collection, Madness, Rack and Honey

When is it luck? When is it accident?

The out of control truck and the sinister disease.
Place as a kind of capture, wind and water blowing
chaos, fire lusting for green.
Also, collision of love and temperament.
Season and need. We sleep
and wake, walk the hours with our eyes
open, gathering what might serve to clarify.
I turn too soon or not at all in the final days
of a long winter, leaving me with nothing
but a suite of bruises. Imagine the great hand
plucking this particular soul, prayers trailing off,
shadows folded, then disappeared.
A tidiness to ruin. I might not have made the trip
or stopped to taste the fresh honey from the pale girl
with the moon face who could only manage a slight, forced smile.
I might have rushed, hapless, into the black sea.

About the Author

Mercedes Lawry grew up in Pittsburgh and after a few peripatetic years post-college, landed in Seattle in the late '70s. She is the author of three poetry chapbooks, the latest, *In the Early Garden with Reason,* was selected by Molly Peacock for the 2018 WaterSedge Chapbook Contest. She's published widely in such journals as *Poetry, Nimrod, Prairie Schooner,* and *Alaska Quarterly Review.* She's also published short fiction, essays, and stories and poems for children. Among her favorite memories are living in the forest in Northern California and washing Margaret Atwood's dishes.

KELSAY BOOKS

www.kelsaybooks.com